The Life Cycle of a

Bee

by Lisa Trumbauer

Consulting Editor: Gail Saunders-Smith, Ph.D.

Consultant: Gary A. Dunn, M.S.,
Director of Education,
Young Entomologists' Society

Pebble Books

an imprint of Capstone Press
Mankato, Minnesota

Pebble Books are published by Capstone Press
151 Good Counsel Drive, P.O. Box 669, Mankato, Minnesota 56002
http://www.capstone-press.com

1 2 3 4 5 6 07 06 05 04 03 02

Library of Congress Cataloging-in-Publication Data
Trumbauer, Lisa, 1963–
      The life cycle of a bee / by Lisa Trumbauer.
      p. cm.—(Life cycles)
      Summary: Simple text and photographs present the life cycle of the bee.
      Includes bibliographical references (p. 23) and index.
      ISBN 0-7368-1450-7 (hardcover)
      1. Bees—Life cycles—Juvenile literature. [1. Bees.] I. Title. II. Life cycles
(Mankato, Minn.)
QL565.2 .T78 2003
595.79′9—dc21   2002001225

Note to Parents and Teachers

The Life Cycles series supports national science standards related
to life science. This book describes and illustrates the life cycle
of a honey bee. The images support early readers in understanding
the text. The repetition of words and phrases helps early readers
learn new words. This book also introduces early readers to
subject-specific vocabulary words, which are defined in the Words
to Know section. Early readers may need assistance to read some
words and to use the Table of Contents, Words to Know, Read
More, Internet Sites, and Index/Word List sections of the book.

Table of Contents

Photographs in this book show the life cycle of a honey bee.

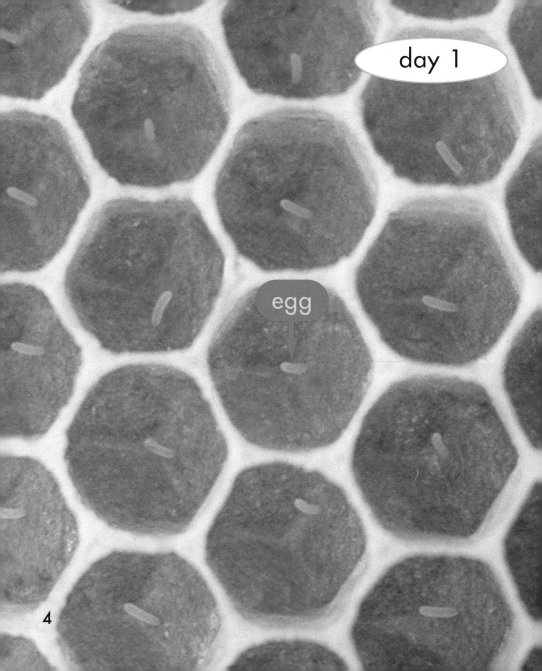

A bee begins life as
an egg in a hive. Hives
have thousands of cells.
Each cell holds one egg.

day 4

larva

A larva hatches from
the egg after three days.
Female bees feed the larva.

8

The larva grows quickly.
It looks like a short,
fat worm.

day 14

pupa

The larva spins a cocoon inside its cell. It becomes a pupa.

day 21

adult

The pupa becomes an adult after one week. The bee leaves its cell. Bees can live for six weeks.

14

Most bees are worker bees.
These female bees make
honey and honeycombs.
Other bees are drones.
Drones are male bees.

queen bee

Some bees are queen bees. Only one queen bee lives in a hive.

queen bee →

The queen bee mates with the drones. She lays one egg in each cell of the hive.

larva

egg

pupa

adult

20

The egg is the start
of a new life cycle.

(Words to Know

adult—the fourth stage of the bee life cycle; an adult is able to mate.

cell—a small section in the honeycomb of a hive; cells have six sides.

cocoon—a silk covering that protects a young bee

drone—a male bee that mates with the queen bee; drones do not work in hives.

hive—the home of a group of bees

larva—the second stage of the bee life cycle; a larva looks like a short, fat worm.

life cycle—the stages of life of an animal; the life cycle includes being born, growing up, having young, and dying.

mate—to join together to produce young

pupa—the third stage of the bee life cycle

queen bee—an adult female bee that lays eggs; only one queen bee lives in a hive.

worker bee—a female bee that feeds larva, gathers pollen, and makes honey; as many as 50,000 worker bees live in a hive.

Read More

Allen, Judy. *Are You a Bee?* Backyard Books. New York: Kingfisher, 2001.

Brimner, Larry Dane. *Bees.* A True Book. New York: Children's Press, 1999.

Heinrichs, Ann. *Bees.* Nature's Friends. Minneapolis: Compass Point Books, 2002.

Schaefer, Lola M. *Honey Bees and Hives.* Honey Bees. Mankato, Minn.: Pebble Books, 1999.

Internet Sites

Bee Anatomy
http://www.pbs.org/wnet/nature/
alienempire/multimedia/bee.html

The Honey Expert
http://www.honey.com/kids/facts.html

Tales from the Hive
http://www.pbs.org/wgbh/nova/bees

Index/Word List

adult, 13
cell, 5, 11, 13, 19
cocoon, 11
drone, 15, 19
egg, 5, 7, 19, 21
female, 7, 15
grows, 9
hatches, 7
hive, 5, 17, 19
honey, 15

honeycomb, 15
larva, 7, 9, 11
life cycle, 21
male, 15
mates, 19
pupa, 11, 13
queen, 17, 19
spins, 11
worker, 15
worm, 9

Word Count: 136
Early-Intervention Level: 15

Editorial Credits
Martha E. H. Rustad, editor; Kia Adams, cover designer; Jennifer Schonborn, interior
    designer; Wanda Winch, photo researcher; Karen Risch, product planning editor

Photo Credits
Brand X Pictures, cover (left)
Bruce Coleman Inc./Kim Taylor, 10, 16, 20 (right)
DigitalVision, 14, 20 (bottom)
Minden Pictures/Konrad Wothe, 18
Stephen McDaniel, 1, 6
Visuals Unlimited/R. Williamson, cover (right); R. Williamson and L. J. Connor, 4, 20
    (left); L. J. Connor, 8, 20 (top); E. S. Ross, 12